T0131416

Together and by Ourselves

Together and by Ourselves

Alex Dimitrov

COPPER CANYON PRESS

PORT TOWNSEND, WASHINGTON

Cover art: Francesca Woodman, *Untitled* (Rome, Italy). Courtesy George and Betty Woodman.

Copper Canyon Press is in residence at Fort Worden State Park in Port Townsend, Washington, under the auspices of Centrum. Centrum is a gathering place for artists and creative thinkers from around the world, students of all ages and backgrounds, and audiences seeking extraordinary cultural enrichment.

LIBRARY OF CONGRESS CATALOGING-IN-PUBLICATION DATA
Names: Dimitrov, Alex, author.
Title: Together and by Ourselves / Alex Dimitrov.
Description: Port Townsend : Copper Canyon Press, 2017.
Identifiers: LCCN 2016047971 (print) | LCCN 2016048360 (ebook) | ISBN
   9781556595103 (paperback) | ISBN 9781619321694 (E-book)
Subjects: | BISAC: POETRY / American / General.
Classification: LCC PS3604.I4648 A6 2017 (print) | LCC PS3604.I4648 (ebook) |
   DDC 811/.6--dc23
LC record available at https://lccn.loc.gov/2016047971

Copper Canyon Press
Post Office Box 271
Port Townsend, Washington 98368
www.coppercanyonpress.org

Contents

III

IV

V

This book is for Nicky Pavlov

I see you in the darkest part of the water and swim

...so long alone together. Alone together so much shared.

Samuel Beckett

Together and by Ourselves

You Were Blond Once

I have a photograph…
when I describe it, you'll know.
On a long train ride they sat and said nothing.
In a pocket, a ticket stub of two hours on a night five years ago.
If you left your life, what life would you leave for? Tell me.
A lot of terrible things used to make me happy.
For years, my friend looked for the perfect chair,
that space he wanted to be in.
Found it two summers ago—never sits in it.
They sat in the back of the restaurant
so he could be upset privately and in public.
You know those streets that have two names,
one before and one after they intersect with another?
How sometimes we can't find them on maps.
Well, I got lost every day that summer in London.
It's the kind of film you want to see by yourself,
but take a car home, don't get lost on me.
None of this is important—and still—
I have a photograph of you…
when we ate an orange in bed.
What month was that in? What did you want from me?
Every book is a book, is a thing you feel by yourself.
You are here. I am alone in this poem.
The window open all day: rain on the white desk, wood floor,
that strange curve on the back of your head (only I knew).
Sometimes I go outside just to feel movement.
Is that why you live here?
Did you imagine your life would turn out this way?
It takes the way someone asks a question to know
if you really want to know them.
You were blond once. So handsome.

And the streets kept their names, and that restaurant closed
and I found the right film when I needed nothing.
Where is he going with this? *Where were you?*
How you approached the water and never went in it.
I'm telling you it's not cold. It's not cold anymore.
Today it's perfect out there. The tea's tea,
there's work, pills, unsent messages, empty glasses.
A lot of things to say with one body (unlikely).
It wasn't that long ago.
I have a photograph of you from that day…

I

Together and by Ourselves

I opened the window so I could hear people.
Last night we were together and by ourselves.
You. You look and look at *Diver*
for Crane by Johns and want to say something.
In the water you are a child without eyes.
Yesterday there was nothing on the beach
and no one knows where it came from.
There's a small animal lodged somewhere inside us.
There are minutes of peace.
Just the feel. Just this once. Where does the past,
where should the period go?
What is under the earth followed them home.
The branch broke. It broke by itself. It did break, James.
We were there and on silent. We were delete, shift, command.
Slow—in black—on an orange street sign.
Missing everywhere and unwritten—suddenly—all at once.
Him. He misses a person and she is still living.
I haven't missed you for long and you are so gone.
Then he stepped away from the poem midsentence…
we must have been lonely people to say those things then.
But there are rooms for us now and sculptures to look at.
In the perfect field someone has left everything
including themselves. You. You should stay here.
It's a brutal and beautiful autumn.
With his hands in the sand, on the earth, under time
he touched something else.
People are mostly what they can't keep and keeps them.
And inside the cage of the Ferris wheel you saw the world.
In the steam, on the mirror: you wrote *so so so…*
so if you're looking for answers you're looking
at every water tower around here.

Why does the sea hold what it loves most below?
Fear. Hopeless money. All the news and the non-news.
How could anyone anywhere know us? What did we make?
And the leather of your chair…it has me marked
so good luck forgetting. The world was a home.
It was cruel. It was true. It was not realistic.
Make sure you date and sign here then save all the worn things.
Because everyone wants to know when it was,
how it happened—say something about it.
How the night hail made imprints all over.
Our things. Our charming and singular things.

Always

We're good at keeping how we shouldn't feel.
On the ferry to the island I burned alone that way.
At least, he thought, there'll be an earth to sink in.
The last scenes in Shakespeare I forget to breathe.
When history caught up with us: no less cruel than our parents.
Wanted to tell you of the psychic witch who found my life with one eye
though we weren't speaking then and here you're dead.
I've put a period to end each thought that won't end.
Come into my house (they were) and talk to me about another life.
The park is true and in perpetual August. Yes, I'm late
and going, going back there.
These small hopes. Traces. Spit on the sidewalk.
I'm an adult and feel less urgent every day.
No one's number matters but the voices anchor;
and the coolness at the bottom of a memory
or how people stop to watch the moon together.
Finally knowing you, I know I cannot know you.
This body's terrible at your religion.
And why eternal life if pleasure's time-bound
and each new year's a killing…
he said, *the dead are one long summer.*
Walking, going nowhere
and some punctuation in an emailed note
reminds me who I am more so than what I've written.
I would pause for you and be a million commas.
The way a flock of birds will leave a tree.
Not just the sound or lifting.
That's where I want to put my hands inside you.
And I found it on a train, beside lit pools,
passing mountains near the city dust
between the ribs or where the dusk waits.

I gave my life a real nice show.
And then you went away so I could see you
as graffiti in a bar just once.
A man is stepping on the moon.
The earth or your one life is gone.
The phone rings in your leaving.
Let your black hair, let your black hair
get in my way always.

Seduction and Its Immediate Consequences

One April in autumn you were my story for hours.
The silence of those days became like a shirt.
"His screaming fits were nothing other than
attempts at seduction," writes Freud in "The Wolfman."
How many accounts for how many things and what did we own?
In the movie of their lives there were people
they saw like notes in the margins
and in the vials a bright mess they carried inside.
Michael, Michael, Michael.
If a name is said enough times in a poem
something will happen. But that isn't your name
and it isn't a city, so where do you live?
Winter taught me to wear a very thin nothing those evenings.
When the car sped through the tunnel, when the cemetery
filled with the living, when the drink was named
for what they couldn't quite taste.
And you didn't decide on the friends or the lovers,
the shoes or the card that was sent and said
come—it's a party for all of our questions.
And why shouldn't we have it.
Why not invite what no one can have.
Immediately, he could tell. Even in the middle of the water.
Soon it will all close without warning or lights.
And between the acts, where we live,
after a while you're wearing too much
no matter what you take off.
But you, filling the room with smoke,
trying hard to be human—
I love you and it's cinema to keep looking.
Listen, I would say in my messages…

on a page or a screen, through a window.
I'd follow you home but it's a very brief night.

Champagne

Lucky or not, we were riding in cars through the seasons.

I read you Baudelaire. *I have more memories than a thousand years.*

And our skin began to look like a puzzle

despite lighting or pleasures.

Columbus Circle at midnight.

Turn around and remind me how late in these photos

you look like an Andrew or prince.

There is fog by the bed and house weather I live in.

Then by dawn I'm a fold in the fabric's small play.

Believe me, he said, every hand finds the right door without keys.

A neck in a low blouse.

So tempting. Now raining.

This waiting for calm that feels more like a drug or a phase.

How bizarre then to show up and stay in this faulty material.

My eyes or your legs or these lips. Do not wince.

Calm your face with another's. You're meant to. It's safer.

All the days have turned up and like models won't change.

What's the evidence then if I'm given receipts

but can't make out what's missing.

I'm still here. One more sip.

One more drag then drag me.

Pull over.

Wherever you park it's the law, you must pay.

We are known when we're walking our bodies

on Mondays and weekends.

J'ai plus de souvenirs que si j'avais mille ans.

Who'd believe that what ends here continues,

it's senseless. Don't listen.

Use up all the memory. Use up all that's there.

Cocaine

People disappear.
And go looking for a place to be looked at.
All the way down Wilshire and above us: like a sheet of indigo tile.
As we waited, our nicotine glowed in the distance like flies
to some heaven, some high road.
"Who sat on mountaintops in cars reading books aloud to the canyons?"
Like gods and at home being extras at best.
I almost believed love then someone new called me
and time's been repeating. Time's on like a show.
They say we're all wanted for living, that somebody's coming,
but even the darkest of frames makes a face feel unsafe.
Yours was here, yours was seen
and it could have been two but you sold it for nothing.
Goodbye to all that then we're back low,
trying to fit the right size for what passes as days.
Take a vitamin, angel. Drink water.
The earth is a big thing.
Would you still like to have it or take the check early tonight?
I get worried then go for a drive with my eyes closed
right here—on the thirty-third floor of my thirty-third year—
what a party it turned out to be.
No one wanted to leave.
When the car you steer best is not yours; or the body.
The house and the job. Rooms of white lines. Gold lobbies.
We cringe at these lists but without them, who's counting?
I was flying over the country with you,
over states in their neat squares and fixed laws.
Flying over the country with women and men
in their trim suits and skirts.
Some nights I wait right out front for a moment
well after I get home. (Forced silence.)

I know what's inside.
We know what comes next.

Chance Visitors

They're all only chance visitors.
By the West Side Highway all summer lighting old fires.
From New York to California, California to New York,
what you told me looks nothing like water or ice.
People change their lives, people change their lives
and the world stays the same.
With the trees tonight (and inside them a century)
by the sailboat pond (and no one knew what you were).
Long mornings: you pass yes.
White nothing: someone should be happy for you.
The main dish, I admit, was a little bit bloody.
That year he shortened his hair many days.
One of us is angry, one of us remains so
neither one remains or keeps this look long.
Every umbrella I've lost was stolen by a stranger, he told me.
The nice ones, the awful: you pay the same thing.
Like a woman who walked up to the shoreline today,
put a chair down and looks like she's still there. She's still now.
Or when you're tired of having the same thing
(when the sun burns your shy skin)
come make your mistakes like you're used to. With me.
Because there's an hour here everyone speaks of and won't name.
Where the light moves past the Pacific
and arrives somewhere low, somewhere under your feet.
It's human to want the sky with you everywhere.
Inside your apartment. Inside the inside life.
And however I say it, the last sentence
sounds better if spoken, not here. By a stone street,
in another city, they're older and trying the same.
I want to know "why" all the time—even now—about everything.
The years come and they're numbers. They have nothing to say.

Today

Today in your hours above the earth
you have questions
that won't trouble you inside it.

Affairs

As if to appear in the months and what follows
is to do something major: a marriage, new city,
the end of a life with someone.
Is it lucky to live or embarrassing?
In the meeting on budget and profit
no one had much to say about that.
I see you in the garden light and after;
taking off your shirt, tipping my head back,
while the clock is like a painting in the background.
It never stops, it never rests.
Under the surface of the lake all the fish
became countless shades of blue rust.
The oars threaded through both water and air.
And I'm supposed to choose who I live with,
and I'm supposed to choose how to live.
Above the ground, through the clouds
this delay on the earth once.
By the midnight-tinged bowties
with my useless, impractical needs.
If I could return anything while I'm here,
where would I look for who wants it?
Sleeping through oil and gold
in a dream of the world without people.
It's hard to imagine but look, it was true once.
Boys in the Pines, fires in the Grove
where I walked everywhere barefoot.
Fasting and gluttony. Minor and more so.
The dirt that won't tire of us and an afternoon
spent but still going on somewhere.
And there was a peach out of season.
Like I imagine we live.

The 25th Hour

Before I took his picture I asked Matthew
to think of one thing he couldn't refuse.
He returned a phone call. I took his picture.
And with us the earth moved at just over 1,000 miles.
What are the eyes and how do they choose…
me in your white shirt. The kitchen lemon. A cuff link.
A wineglass on top of a book in a bed.
When it's too much, I smoke a cigarette inside the apartment.
When the trains empty (around three in the morning),
I don't want to sit.
The Carlyle lights up and for someone it's Wednesday
when truly it's past that.
What is the mind and how do I choose…
you in my white shirt. The hair parted over or back still.
Severely. The doctor wants three to four vials
and thinks that he knows me.
I like that. I like him.
Exiled on earth amid the shouting crowds.
She would slip through the service entrance on 77th
and up there the president waiting…
he thinks that he knows her.
We're here and in color but black and white suits us.
She liked that. She liked him.
And after millions of years (or 200 nearly),
the day turns out longer. A twenty-fifth hour of secrets.
A twenty-fifth hour without you.
I think I've had plenty of glasses and lemons
though lately I want more.
Exilé sur le sol au milieu des huées.
It could not have been anything else. It was this.

The 13th Month

A little of our misplaced lives,
we saw them waving on the roof in the dark
and thought they were birds.
Who you were underneath the umbrella.
In the best of memory no one has a real part.
Part of it, he kept thinking, is to try and say something
of what everyone brought instead of themselves.
Like that hour you were more of a person than had been in years.
Because it was eyes, mouth, and less real—more senseless;
nothing the hands can take back. You'll excuse me
while I write it all like a postcard. You'll excuse me,
I went to the thirteenth month of the year looking for you.
No matter the matter he was found in mostly low places.
He was birds. He was bird.
And lately, lately seems a place in time
that's happening never and always.
Lately I've taken to two of you like a pill or a fruit.
Some of life. Some more choices.
(He tried them. I tried you.)
Unforgivable but drawn to red things.
And while not entirely about us, we attended our lives.
We stayed. And stayed longer. Then, he said,
when you look at the snow…who do you think of?
"It all seems impossible, but so real. There are witnesses."
On the back of a photograph, one by Felix Gonzalez-Torres.
Like days when I wait for myself to return.
What I mean, where I went; we're all missing.
You'll understand if I write it all like a postcard.
I have nowhere to send it but here—
written for you—and too soon.

Poem with William

Looking for the news, I found the blue corridor
where nothing happens. It was blue.
We just kissed.
And because I took you there you were quiet.
It seems people are everywhere and so few.
A hand has five fingers. Five fingers and five thousand wants.
Seemingly endless. This defense of obsession.
How the cars, they did carry us.
In the plane we were what asked to go far.
Soon could mean anytime, any way…and like all of it
nothing was soon. Soon was no thing.
Our mouths were small gifts in the distance.
We were seen: so high up and withdrawn—
which is where you would like to remember,
which is how it all tastes.
I do feel you, pressing against a stranger for so long
and it was my own bones after all.
He admired how the child would not answer the question.
He admired how he told of the day without us.
It's a small room in the back where we're going.
The truth is, I'm wearing a black belt
and nothing grips quite like you do.
It's possible to get the news from poems,
impossible to say what we are.
Every day on the way to the last one
I think: description is useless.
And still someone had to describe it.
To make it less cold, to unmake what was already there.
Without photographs. Without headlines.
It's difficult to see the world from the world.

And it's true. We were in it.
With these partial and unlikely days.

Lifetime

There must be ways to delay the past
from so frequently arriving. Shoes on the bed,
keys inside the coat not meant for seasons.
Someone's body is a bomb
inside their well-built home.
Suit days. Full days. Less days.
Drama. Comedy. Opera.
Dress nights. Fall nights. All night.
Prose. Verse. Prose—
the costly comma.
Hold on, one more thing then:
one minute, one second,
almost there, right on time,
5 late, 10 late, so late,
walking now, walking past,
on it, by it, in the back, toward the front,
right around, right beside,
right behind—finally here,
finally done, finally with you.
Do you see me?
Do you see this? Do you see us?
Do you see?

The Hall of Mirrors

So then I pressed myself to one window after another
and saw where the image began.
I walked through the rooms with all of the people…
their black shawls, sharp collars, small hearts.
And before the last hour of getting together
they asked if we wanted a drink or a story,
a polish or chip in the paint. *Yes*, I said.
I'll have both. I'll have many. I'll have more than a lot.
And did we talk about love? I think we talked about love.
Did we stay late in our leaving? I remember that too.
You swam in the ocean. I walked on the earth.
The hall of mirrors was empty.
Our eyes played guests for the night.
And now, before the obvious ending
I've somehow come up to the roof. Here
where our voices sound indistinct, almost impossible.
Who would think (I left without telling anyone)
it was ever just us.

II

Famous and Nowhere

Life is like Los Angeles. Bright and disappointing.
I watched you closely on the pier that wasn't home.
They grew up in parking lots once and now they are stories;
speeding and smoking through yesterday's games.
Past the stone angel heads and over the calm brutes,
the freeway thins and wears white like a patient tonight.
I get lost on the way but I always return here.
Once I'd like to be left and unheard from.
I'd like to be nothing.
LA woman, Sunday afternoon.
Take off your jeans, put on a curse.
When in the evenings you fill that one glass
in the mornings you feel it.
The sun's been a sun for four billion years.
So on these obvious screens where I'm with you
it does get religious. The billboards keep selling us love
when the people are too hard to find.
Patrick, Lucas...I must be forgetting.
I do live without you.
The moon's been a moon and for no one, four billion ways.
Still...I remember driving up Mulholland in August,
no phone calls or questions. No faces.
You said, "if anyone knows where we are,"
if there's photos but nothing to show here.
Life's like LA.
It's famous and nowhere.
Leaving town I sat next to a senseless and beautiful boy
who asked where I live.
His unwashed hair or the way his eyes were just eyes...
the soul is a tiring thing. You can have it.

I don't know what you mean's what I told him.
It's more simple than that. I'm just passing through.

The Standard

When we sit down D says, "I just down them."
The foyer is dark. You wouldn't see anyone coming for you.
If they were, if we are; going backwards and forwards
over the bridges, into the same sinking beds.
We want to know what it feels like to die
but we don't want to die.
You wanted me happy, *come happy*,
and now that I'm happy—now what?
I need you to check your eyes
and make sure you're seeing this clearly
when you're seeing me often
in stairwells, hotel rooms, the car or these bars.
Last month you tell me, *I'm ready for spring too*,
spring comes and I tell you, *I'm ready for fall*.
Ready for summer. Ready for one more new season
to take up my body and stay.
Don't be kind to the body.
It's just one more body.
Not once was it kindness that stayed on the menu
with people like us.
I'm on my fourth now, he's on his third.
Look the foyer stays dark here.
Your mother goes quiet.
Our fathers arc all the way
going and going then gone.
One cigarette I smoked on the roof of The Standard,
I didn't even finish it. Transfixed by all of that water,
the hundreds of cars and the ways people take themselves out.
And however true, to whoever had gone up there with me,
I said *lucky life*. That no one gets to return to the past.
No matter our tedious days of ambition, no matter the nights.

The nights, the nights—
these endings we've learned to stay up for.
The flaws we recall and regret
when our tricks stop to work.

The Last Luxury, JFK Jr.

Born of the sun, we traveled a short while toward the sun.
Where there were seasons and sky. Where there were monuments.
Like a single-engine plane in a July haze.
Or our nights that pile up like shoes in a guest room.
I would talk about the weather when I'm in the right weather but when.
At the Stanhope Hotel, just hours before, they were people.
The Navy divers found them lying under one hundred and sixteen feet of waves.
Or a small body of water meeting a new, larger body.
Healthy body. Nobody. We just couldn't decide.
Spatial disorientation occurs when you don't refer to your instruments
and begin to believe the whatever inside you.
When I punished the Austrian roses by forgetting about them
I knew that they couldn't keep beauty and they couldn't keep time.
The day of his father's funeral: November 25, 1963, was also his third birthday.
Then—sometimes: the urge for new windows.
A color other than black for the best days.
In fourteen seconds plummeting at a rate beyond the safe maximum.
The safe maximum at the office, bedroom, or bar.
On the way there, somewhere between floors, no velocity could recover us.
And again. Sometimes the right music,
sometimes lucky to be in good light.
Once a week I go into a room and pretend to have similar interests.
Every day I wake up and brush to the left.
We're the good people, the bad people and the people we aren't.
Socialite, journalist, lawyer. Americans. These Americans.
They always button their coats when they see luck.
Dear Johnny boy, thanks for asking me to be your mother
but I'm afraid I would never do her justice.
My eyebrows aren't thick enough for one.
But you know, it was like eating the best grapefruit.
Being here. Here (and then what).

"…yet once you start answering those questions…where do you stop?"
The old photograph of a young salute.
That one send-off to death, family; the beginning of character.
Maybe you know it's the last year of the century. So come late and leave early.
(Others flying similar routes reported no visual horizon.)
It's the last luxury. To go early and never come back.

Lindsay Lohan

It's a cold rehearsal before we all drive off.
The ride out is mindless and short on goodbyes.
And in the flurry of parties she lost her passport.
A slow smoke, a think in the old car…
how they moved through their places and phrases
and on to the bedroom where mostly we kept it all in.
People won't tell you, but if you lose enough things you do become something.
All day the water endlessly filters so it's not the same pool.
In the morning our photos looked darker than us
and the subject we were was a gamble (I know).
The night winds came through and the gin took it well.
Voyeur. Soho House. No one told us about us.
I don't remember, but you wanted me happy or loose like your change?
Because it's not written here or it's not written well
and the boys flitted out of the Aero like men do.
From one to two I saw three. No mistake. Nothing but getting undressed.
And then you. They said you sped through those hills and would not stop.
They said you had nothing to say in Marina del Rey.
Reno—Monroe—1960. *I know all these lines, John.*
I promise you I do. Yes, baby, we know that.
And Cook, presumably speaking to Huston, said kindly on the recorder:
"We must have 86,000 feet of sound film by now."
So tonight, we'd like to invite only you to this soft light.
It could be your first time, it could be a waste.
Her arm was full of bracelets, one of which, she said, had been given to her by S.
And sometimes I think: I'm at this dinner forever.
It's like home. I don't leave without paying something.
When they wrote about you and you showed your tattoos,
everyone had grown tired but they were tired without you.
It was late on some coast where you walked and for now it was quiet.

The gulls couldn't tell what we were so they stared. They kept watching. Pretend otherwise but we just couldn't stop.

Los Angeles, NY

What he can't remember is why soon they'll stop meeting
in the gold, lonely rooms. Through the old streets, through history,
the limousine came and inside it you flipped like a page in a cheap paperback.
The ride into death glowed past summer
and the end took a long time to write—mostly descriptive:
peeling away the fruit's meat and the smell still under your nails.
Like a scarf, the adjectives barely covered us.
Although it was beautiful, the dialogue revealed little about anyone else.
"We are not just those persons which we were,"
wrote John Donne, and it was a question.
How love disappeared like money,
and you ran the asylum inside you alone...

American Money

Perhaps this was one way through being here:
the lists, the lanes; the pills, the days.
You don't scream but occasionally sit in the shower.
Everything people won't say to each other
covers the walls of rest stops for years.
Patrick, you never call.
A new shirt or bedroom, some known shift;
"whatever it looks like," you're telling the doctor,
your mother, the doorman—"I don't want to know."
The fashion is everyone's loosely committed to something,
it drives the mind wild. To lose, yes,
and also to keep any one thing (with all things)
in any one life (would you try all this twice?).
You take yourself uptown to see all the paintings.
You take yourself downtown to take yourself up.
"Between scotch and nothing, I'll take scotch," said Faulkner.
Between nothing and nothing, it may be there's this.
And the wrong kind of gazing can halt conversation.
Our being at funerals is perfectly planned and polite.
You don't know this but yes, I watched the boy in Miami
drop bills from his hands and I did want to keep him.
Hair in his face, jeans almost off.
That year, on a plane with a woman terrified of flying,
I talked her through all of the stalling, the going,
once in a while rehearsed lying, once in a while
here we are. We arrived.
At the end of a trip, in another punishing city.
Perhaps people pay for most things. The lost keys or court papers.
Yet no one had a check for the guilt or that weekend
no matter how often, how quaintly we asked.

American Nothing

Tonight the wind tears through a flag
building a religion from cruelty.
Someone lifts his face out of privacy, out of death.
I'm here to marry you, lonely American nothing—
with my useless name and your aimless car
ready to take me out of myself. If the body was harmless,
history would read lighter and we'd take our drinks long.
I can smell your hair from here and it's years after.
Below my window boys eat chocolate with their fingers
and the taste of their cheap sweetness keeps me awake.
Even now the voice on your radio takes me home
where I never lived. The question I sleep with
grips stronger than any stranger that finds me.
What do we want when we ruin each other?
I've done terrible things and I still want to know.

Jesus in Hollywood

It's three days past Easter and at the light on Fountain
one car behind me is Jesus. He's driving a white BMW
and he is alone. I drive slow and keep an eye on the mirror
wondering if I'm the only one who sees him,
making a list of the awful things I've done
this year, should he pull me over.
Jesus, I abandoned my longest relationship
and wasn't sorry. Not sure I am now.
I stopped talking to my mother
then started (and stopped again after),
so these days I'm not sure who's talking to whom
even when we are screaming or silent.
Like you, I kept coming back to Hollywood.
I wanted to believe in life after death
and if it's true anywhere—surely then—here.
I tried to be alone and with people
and both almost killed me.
Then I almost killed me:
drinking in a bungalow in Venice (July),
reading the tabloids and Milton,
buying myself two hours with another bottle of wine
then buying myself more with a book
even longer than *Paradise Lost*.
Jesus, they probably think you are glamorous.
Look at the car you're driving. It's a beautiful rental.
You should stay in your price range.
They probably think you are lucky and set.
Maybe too young and mysterious. Just imagine.
Who wouldn't let you in if you knocked on his door?
And who wouldn't cry with you
in a parking lot outside any American mall?

Do you even cry, Jesus? Do you even pay rent?
Would you live in the world that we do?
Or do you just like to drive, see the sights,
keep your sunglasses on, keep the real you inside:
a white BMW on Fountain. Or wherever it is we are now,
I'm going to let you pass me.
I'm not going to follow you, Jesus.
I'm going back to the sun and the people,
back where I never belonged.

Elvis in New York

Time stopped and everyone was seventeen.
For a moment, you thought, why get out of my seat.
There they were: walking in the streets
like a lake caught running in a house.
One in the morning. You in the evening.
It was Friday, June 9, 1972.
He wore a golden cloak,
you dressed for one more Friday in the world.
There are many places that I haven't been, he said.
Like I've never played New York.
Somewhere in a place like here there's more than people.
Sometimes with you, I don't know who'd think about the dead.
Manhattan, you're more beautiful than any man on any morning.
Between nine and midnight if you cross the avenue you're someone new.
What was it, they asked, that made him try this.
Why relive the same known highs?
Like a question at the bottom of a pillbox,
(one you shouldn't answer)
I just missed it, he said flatly. *There are many places.*
There are many places that I haven't been.
And with that, the flags along Eighth blustered.
City papers sent their crews.
It's the bright nights we remember,
those that live outside the hours
like a show in early summer, or a vision at the Garden;
knowing nothing of our narrative.
Once in a great while, the *Times* had written,
the way a thing is done becomes more important than the thing itself.
So there they were again. Returning.
To the walls where they had hung things.

To required love. The record playing in a room and ending.
Like a life someone once had.

July Fourth

On one of them and rather unforeseen,
walking across a roof still full of people
perhaps to find someone or smoke
with the New Yorker sign in view—
a friend soon getting married and another
leaving the country to start over—
I remember the late suburban echo
of the television's flicker
one teenage summer watching videos
of Greg Louganis dive in 1984,
the same year I was born
though I'm not there yet (in the world)
or on that platform in LA,
his body in the air
what I sometimes imagine to be
freedom: unattainable state of being—
and even in the replay, in slow motion,
the brevity of his freedom hurts me
in a way I can't admit, not then
when I was just a boy, or on a roof
and looking up at thirty-one,
fireworks on all sides
of the night—and the sky—
do I not love the sky
although I'm seldom there?—
and if that's true why not today
or on occasion think
that freedom might be real, that somehow
someone got there once;
even for seconds, moments, fantasy.

Speeding Down the FDR

Dressing himself in the cab for one room then another.
The new fame on the radio playing—past the cathedrals,
toward the young graves after that.
In the dusk, they sold flowers to everyone
stopped at our red light. In this life you're far.
Like the sun appears to the water when late.
All those people you see, all the hallways you drink in;
through tunnels and traffic—you might wear a tie,
you might keep your shoes on forever today.
Let them photograph your soul, says Jimmy.
Memorize your alleys, take yourself back home.
Already we're here and already we're through it.
The toll's blinking wildly at you.
They'll stop you from smoking indoors, they'll arrest you.
But no one can stop you from kissing the wrong kind of men.
Up ahead, a police car lights up like a kids fair.
The phone in my hand won't keep still.
Maybe it's you and you're driving the wrong way;
a feeling you hailed once.
Something to steer you toward me then away.
If the shirt's fitted well, ten blocks and it's off you.
If the light starts to bother, let it grow darker still.
I was speeding down the FDR one night,
it was August and heavy.
I am speeding down the FDR tonight,
it is April and dead. Who would drive himself away?
There's a stranger who's doing it for me.
Who would drive herself below?
Like a bath in street clothes.
Eyes on the throat, money counted to zero.

And everyone's cleaned up like heaven.
Believe it. Everyone's dressed down for hell.

Speeding Down PCH

Almost arriving, I've gone somewhere else.
You threw so much of yourself getting where,
going far, like the waves growing restless
in a white convertible speeding down PCH.
Who could lie? It's still such a pleasure and panic
to wake up alone, unable to answer
one person instead of two.
I arrange the pills into hearts, spread them over the desk:
we are not mathematics.
When the waiter tells me his name
it's the part of the meal I like most.
I am never coming back.
Even if the setting is different, even if the plan
is to speed through it twice. A vase—some familiar face
instead of a clock on a mantel.
A video of a person with both hands in his hair.
I come to your door, get you off,
watch you shave in the morning.
Through the hurry (inside the waiting)
I realize the director is someone who doesn't show up.
Like the end of the day, I am orange for more
and in minutes I go dark.
What you'll find is our lives are addictions:
money, love, gossip. Gossip, love, work.
And if the video plays as it should,
both hands do come down.
The hair's going any which way and the gaze
can't be read—even looking into the camera is dying.
Why fight it. If you die enough times
you become your own saint.

End of Summer

Late afternoon he walks into the Pacific.
A plane spells out an offer that dissolves in the sky.
On the boardwalk a man takes down dictation
from Jesus and reads it to anyone who'll listen
for a negotiable price. *Visit the afterlife*
reads one sign. *Death is an illusion* another.
He likes to swim out and find a place
where voices from the shore
are no longer audible. Surely, he thinks,
like the boardwalk, the afterlife is crowded;
where would anyone find peace there.
A surfer catches the last good waves of the day
and someone blares a boom box while passing.
You only gotta do one thing well
to make it in this world, babe.
And the seagulls scatter then collect themselves
around the same spot; shameless and unknown.
Most of the week goes on like this:
without messages from home, without reason.
The hard hours are to come. They won't
announce themselves with signs or music.
And he decides not to prepare.
For company or anything else.

III

In the New Century I Gave You My Name

The orchestras kept playing. They had a gin fix.
Why in this fog I still see you I can't say.
With your beard and high darkness around me.
In your small machine many messages
and faces that once let you in.
The ocean drowns time all the time, slowly.
Everyone had a birthday and buried something.
I was coming from one person and into another
when really what are we: some accident.
In this show where we all have a favorite.
What we have is a taste for that thing we can feel,
will not say. Some of us wanted more
and in all the wrong ways too.
There was of course an escape…
in a year, on a street, in some near distant past
when what had us was childish and flame.
And maybe it would have been different
and maybe it would have been this.
Do you remember my hair when I met you?
Much longer. The violins ended it well.
Outside, the city continued to tease us.
Hurricanes came, storms couldn't please us:
it was all very fast and beautifully made.
You ask why I'm thinking of death
but I'm thinking of you and it's fleeting.
We were terrible, unrelenting and everywhere then.
All I know is I can't stop writing about people.
So much happened. I can't stop writing about love.

A Living

I watched you row us back, into the distance of human familiars.
And the bees gathered as if to become more than one sound.
In the city, when late, I want even the well-behaved strangers
at boring parties. They exhaust me.
All small talk and posture; (come here and exhaust me)
and what is the mind?
Even you. The leaves. In their temporary dying,
give a rich background to people taking each other to bed.
Why would I give up the physical world?
Today, it is all I believe.
And whatever addictions it sells me
(the first open mouth on my own teenage mouth)—
I am shy but impressed.
I am living and badly. The oars hit the dock,
the plates cling to their places,
look at all that has come here and gladly
to rot. A handful of flowers and vinegar.
Leather and silk. Cancer and love.
I don't even need to be promised fidelity now.
Someone's lowered his hands to a place without speech.
The pelting on the window is rain.
My tongue, I have found, is warmer
than any sentence I've wanted to feel.
And what I have wanted, I should try and forget.
So I stay;
don't you think so—where else would we go,
what is open this late?
I have waited all day just to see you.
In the darkest part of the water.
I see you in the darkest part of the water and swim.

Out of Some Other Paradise

And people walked out of churches and bars,
cafés and apartments, cities, towns, photographs,
someone's Friday night party,
someone they once knew or slept with.
They walked out of meetings and dinners,
out of lives, on each other, on love
and rarely on time.
Some walked out of dark places,
slow places, strange places, places
they wouldn't go back to, places they never did find.
Then did. And walked out again
for the third, fourth, fifth time perhaps.
People walked out through doors
and through letters, through looks across rooms,
gifts that gave nothing of what they withheld,
what they couldn't give back. Then others
just walked out on everything. That was that.
What can be said about what we do to each other.
What street, I don't remember,
on the way to someone's going-away,
I saw you, as if in the middle of a sentence,
snow: your new evening clothes.

The Past Remembers You Differently

I returned with a new way to think about you.
On another page Whitman described what it feels like to live.
The day loosened its intentions. Even these recent errors.
The lights in the street almost speaking.
The terrible more than anyone wants.
And where is that life from a past that can't see you…
what wouldn't we want death to know about us?
Today, he wants to know where to put all the old things.
He wants to know about signs.
If you once signed your name here no one now sees it.
I swallowed some part of the evening
then left and went looking
and looking is where I can follow the plot.
The kids of those years ran back through the fires.
They were here, they were young, they were all
in their faces, their small frames: that's us.
I want to run through my life without asking for anything.
I want to run through my life until I am a word.
This is the nineteenth line of the poem.
I am waiting for you to look at me.
Sun bleaches the paper.
Time slides through the flesh.
Someone on the corner is imprinting the building
with a kind of humanity
just by touching it.
We are often in mirrors and small in this suffering.
This is never enough. And of course I'm still here
waiting for you to look at me.
To bring me the dead leaves
at the bottom of the river.
In the mud of the madhouse.

And the light that breaks open the casket,
stitch it over my eyes.

All the Way Up I Took Myself

There's a little of myself in you, you know it.
Like the night in day, like that feeling
of New York in Paris.
I could say a lot of things,
I could tell you about Venice
or how Turner's paintings make us
much more beautiful
when we're in front of them,
the story of Bulkaen, how he stood,
mouth open, and one by one
a group of boys would spit in it—
how spit will sometimes turn to roses,
how roses turn to nothing.
We're below the fog,
sometimes we're in it
and we try—we try to write or call,
hang up, forget just why
or who we're missing.
Did I tell you? I finally made it
to the Empire State, that building,
all the way up is where I took myself.
It's wild I know, but everyone I love
I saw below, like figurines.
You were walking in the city
in your long black coat
and you felt far and happy.
The rain was red, the rest, unlike
the past, was roses.

Some New Thing

The best reason to live is that there is no reason to live.
I walked to your apartment in the late night.
Flowers I didn't plant began to be flowers
and I was a color and then I was none.
Conrad said, let the train take you anywhere,
pass all the old stops. I let the train take me anywhere,
I passed all the old stops. With you I liked being nowhere
and with you I live nowhere now.
The best reason to paint is that there is no reason to paint.
Keith Haring wrote that. It could be about us.
I go into churches and I go into bars:
I feel the time stop.
To feel—you can't stop at some point.
Not a religious thing. Why on earth or why not.
Let's be in a Sunday morning
with no complacencies of the peignoir,
no late coffee or oranges—all he does
is watch the neighborhood dogs getting walked.
No one will let you through if you don't walk your own sadness.
No one will let you touch if you're a person at all.
One summer we walked the entire island of Manhattan,
we were our own animal.
From Inwood to the water to your small want.
And you. You, you, you
you can read these lines in any order
because I want to leave nothing out
and there's nothing here.
Words are just words. What I feel
I feel twice and risk three of.
Some new thing.
How there's more here without us at all.

All Apologies

When we drove through the canyon toward Taos
I remember feeling relief at not knowing you at all.
We were strangers in a car
and then strangers in a house in the desert.
The gate. And the days no one else lived in.
I think I made a mistake in wanting to be known;
but I came to New York and I stayed.
So the rain now feels like a language for warmth
when it's just like the leaves are:
they fall whether or not you take note.
It's not time to be older but easier to assume so.
Someone I almost married is crossing the street.
We could let a coincidence end us completely.
We're people. The gods know this about us.
I stared at the cracked windshield but found my way
to your hands; in your hair, on the wheel.
Let me be obvious.
There is nothing easy about November or the desert.
You could lose a lot in both.
Sometimes a conversation between people
is a mirror to fix yourself in—a departure.
Who wants to be what they are?
Not the mystics. Not even the saints.
We could be on burial grounds or long beaches.
The arrival of the mildest winter.
Where I stood in a courtyard with tall, marble warriors,
asking them the same question.
Who wants it? Who thinks they'll withstand it and do so.
The windows through which we watch something change
live on highways and bridges with little to show for.
Of course it's all coming.

Let me be obvious.
We're both leaving and here.

Birthday

While the arrangement overwhelmed the blue vase
and died quickly, everyone looked.
In the day-to-day headlines of science and capital
the talk was of water and being beyond this small Earth.
Someone called in to say "many more"
and although it was known what the many would be—
once again—I needed to ask.
How would I know what was mine here and when?
Each one went (as they do)
and was silent in adding its mass and its mark.
As it turned out I slept and then rose and the many were true.
I kept watch of the nights it would rain and the days it was clear.
Until passion grew useless, of course, and the weather would come
as the weather would like, how it all just became what it was
regardless of proof or our planning for more.
What were these lives people had if not
too small to count and still counted like stocks.
A patient outside the waiting room asked for a light.
It's my birthday, he said
and I smiled short but true.
We know too much to smoke and too little for anything else.
That morning another celebrity mess made the papers.
By evening the city forgot to bring us all home.
Like faces we put on at parties for people we won't see,
our eyes they go looking despite who we are.
Something else I became on those birthdays then with you.
Not feeling or figment; not larger than slight.
Every time we fucked without saying more than hello
to each other. Wanting nothing and all things.
The bowl on the desk finally breaking.
Two people astonished and waiting around.

Perfect Day

This late and it seems they've been everything.
The low light of the lobby spreads out like a day.
What are the windows for you? What are the dead-end streets?
I would give you these relics unprompted, without doubt—
but even a strand of hair needs to be looked at and carried and changed.
Watch the man on the balcony settle into his life.
All winter I've done it. And I would be venom
then fire, a true unpaid actor. I do not care to be air.
At Coney Island, on the first of each January
people take off their clothes and watch the Atlantic make room for them.
Even if it was for the obvious beauty—the sentence began—
even if it was all the money and fame.
Who'd ask to stay?
In London Robert is cutting an apple with only his eyes.
The world (yes) is turning. It's like a fast date.
And in the cab's silence I'm loud but not talking,
less young than expected. Less ready or sane.
On that Tuesday (a Midtown billboard
in the graceless morning) all but an X had gone out
and so flickered. Stating the nothing without fear or blame.
In London Robert is closing his eyes by letting his hair grow.
So much blond falling over his wrists.
An earthquake. Another reversal. Do answer.
Are you often surprised with yourself?
Because even here in my body
I waited outside like a stray. Perfect day then
what did you tell me: 8:39 when the sun sets,
5:21 up again. "Oh, but you would,
it's too like you to miss it."
Become less and flee more—that's us.

We're those people.
Catching each other just barely but pleased.

False Spring

Forgive this brief message. It's mostly to say this:
Rachel, I changed my hair, where I live,
changed the way I touch people…
but the balcony plant is still ugly and stubborn.
He will not be loved.
And you were in Paris, while you were in Paris,
everyone mistook him for something else—
even the season. His favorite.
False spring.

Central Park

Now we see each other every day.
As if the buildings had forgiven us
for something done by others once here long ago.
Strangers, spectators, witnesses
and how shy we go round (and the dead going with us)
the Kennedy Onassis Reservoir where it's still summer,
where we appear the same but different to each other in a park.
Late crossings on the Sundays of your small life.
Off of streets, without plan, north of Strawberry Fields.
"An artificial pastoral in the nineteenth-century
English romantic tradition." Performance.
It's still a surprise I keep finding life here.
What a person can have, where desire can sit;
how *to have* must be twice a verb—
it delivers, it makes calls. It won't let the rest of us rest.
But we come for the sun and the cold rain regardless.
We live with the leaves that die fast
and the lamps that go late. If I do know one thing,
there's more fiction around than true people.
Less beasts on their leashes than beasts of our kind.
At dusk, when I leave (which is something I'm good at)
the paths will refashion the way earth hunts time.
Many questions I've hurried through stay here;
unwanted, unasked for. The lawns keep your secrets.
The trees do retrieve us. It's little like dying in fact.
And on the way out, if the park should become you—
this no one told me, this I forgot—
only because its own center escapes sight:
the statues, the wonderland.
Like us, it is seldom all there.

New Year

I know someone who'll watch and won't be touched in bed.
You did not find the news you wanted.
The desert was more than a drive.
I know someone who has the phone one pillow over
like a person, should it ring.
And you can dress yourself for nighttime in the light,
and you can't say more than you have when someone's gone.
What to do now with the ribbons from the old year?
It's just as well I love that one fast hour after parties,
when alone and driving back late
with whatever has been said or done
still playing sharply in the mind.
One peels, one straightens, one does it all over—
it is not / it must be enough.
Bring me the plate with our complaints
arranged so lazily, everyone's forgotten to eat
so they walk through the rooms
looking for someone to sink their teeth in.
It could have been a place quite free
of our attachments and obsessions,
where we decided then to meet—
the first in many months, the last one of its kind.
Some lost place in Manhattan
where we'd never go together when we were once.
The type of haunt we all know well;
the songs are free but nothing else is.
And by some door or window in the front or back,
a faded map of New York State,
Nebraska, California, homebound.
Someone's life is interrupted without promise.
Neither doom nor luck, not funeral or party.

Gentleman's Hour

It's nothing like they expected.
Kennedy is dead. The childhood dog is dead.
On my desk is a lamp with the face of a lion
and rust where its teeth used to be.
People and how they described each other...
incomparable to the sea.
The point in the day when it's no longer morning but memory.
Memory. What did I say to death to excuse myself
for always being somewhere else?
What would they do with all this if love ended before life,
and the trains crossed the earth but never did leave.

IV

Nights with People, Days Without

How could I describe the ending to you?
The streets on the way out were wet.
Floors, bed, walls—impossible not to press against something.
Who called. Who cares. I had a drink by myself at the bar.
A long skirt on the avenue reminded you of your mother.
The scent in the car took him back to a place where he'd left something black.
Every morning is a little different, isn't it—
nights with people, days without.
So they woke up and wanted nothing so close to them.
Nothing next to whatever was there.
Me, I had another drink by myself at the bar.
I don't think we deserve anything for our suffering.
But I have this old self and it's wanting…things, things.
Isn't it funny, he said—no, I can't tell you…
so put your mouth here or leave.
A season, another, no subject with your email
and why language—where we're all mostly helpless—
may be a place to give in and give up on…
being a person. Being a person. Being a person.
With that, the student asked how he should end his poem.
What would help? He asked twice.
Me. Me again. I had a few more drinks by myself at the bar
(and I'm sorry I'll never write back but I'm telling you
here in front of no one and everyone).
Be your own fantasy.
Me. Back to me. I came home to a freezing apartment:
doors, windows, books open. Characters. All of us,
everywhere. I took off my clothes and I was a person.
In a cold room with a dead light.
A subject with no subject line.

Night Call

When we did then go after each other in those most unreasonable hours.
Twice at the Lowell Hotel: bringing you uptown,
bringing you down. Let me walk this situation
and touch each window from within. "I hate funerals.
I'm glad I won't have to go to my own. Only, I don't want one—
just my ashes cast on waves." And that was the beautiful child.
For the short while then, briefly, like the inside of a wrist turned toward you
we forgot we were awful people. Now isn't that nice,
how animals walk toward what calls them by a name no one can give.
Part of the menu, wardrobe, backdrop…
what did we ask for in fact?
Not always will the sun stay where you live.
On some ship that's so far down there, where the elevator stops just once.
Lead us into death now said the priest, and the men all wove it in their hair.
Outside the Spanish Steps we took photographs for everyone who wasn't there.
And I watched a small bird run that yard without its head
so the blood could be a blessing. So you saw someone you love kill something too.
When the head goes there are muscles that keep going.
One of them would call the other if the night called for a smoke.
Remind me then…what is this? Our agreement.
You can watch me while I read you something.
You can have me while I'm here.
Love is difficult for brutes like us, with or without assets.
Agree or disagree?
How the bay made the day feel wide, unlike a tunnel.
My voice had nothing to say after the beep.
Or let me show you: unlimited intimacy
is a kind of poison. So is counting checks or pills or weeks.
And many critics felt he wasted his gifts by going to too many parties
and appearing on too many talk shows.
Yet in some jeweled corridor of their lives

where time was a freedom and hell-mate,
the fish circled, openmouthed, and never left the aquarium.
Every lover is a stranger, every stranger a lover all over again.
So I've been popular and unpopular
(you'll be a body on the earth and in the earth too).
It's mostly the same thing, mostly the same fears.
Voracious and bound. They didn't know it
(and it wasn't a choice) how we're truly impossible.
We had to. They had to live here.

Strangers and Friends

We slept with the doors open one more night.
And now when I try it alone it does not feel the same.
Something about time when it's right there in front of you
disguised as a person. A person disguised as a voice
at the end of its reach. A photo booth strip.
You're more material to me than a house
and I haven't felt much of the weather living inside.
Rain on a mouth. Fingers in dirt.
I wish I had the mind of an orchid or sky.
A childhood beach when it's cold yet not late in the year.
I am leaving you there with the shirts and the shoes thrown about,
waiting to be retrieved by the people who've given them use
and aren't done slapping their bodies against the sea.
Nothing has come to impress me. We leave.
Thrown in the blue of the wet afternoon
where no one can stay without being bled;
we, who are so full of blood.
I am watching you make all the lights.
The Madonna swings across the dashboard,
her face does not change.
And whether it's the mountains of New Mexico
or the streets in this city of lack,
we are driving in the easy silence
of people who do not yet know
what they'll take from each other.
This is the shortest part of the drive,
the part that won't photograph well but seems real.
Soon we'll be stopping at a gas station and a pool
and a diner where no one will eat.
No matter the places I've taken my clothes off

I always keep one thing on. One.

One of us. Asking for more than what's ours.

Tonight

Tonight in your hours away from earth
you have questions
that won't trouble you inside it.

People

On the plane from New York to California
the handsome men sit alone like the past.
I have so much to say to them but don't
and order a scotch—neat. A word
that describes almost nothing.
Your dress in a storm one September.
Ethan's red shoulders coming out of a bath.
Maybe I haven't loved men the way I love women
although often in the afternoons
and now somewhere in the middle of the country,
I want even the bad things to do over.
The wheels coming down right before landing.
The wheels you can feel but don't see.
And the people, how being with people,
has turned out to be, more or less, something like that.

Lines for People after the Party

And whenever they couldn't speak they looked at each other.
How long should I look at the world before I go home?
It's a moody life like Debussy on a weekend
and all the appointments and money and drinks they do go.
So with our beautiful coats we went back to that mess
and what happened? Someone found what they wanted
by night, by mistake. In the car it felt like summer
and we lived with no sun…just metals and leather.
A lot of Mondays. A lot of you in the grass I go to and touch.
Oh and Los Angeles for its slow light. Rome for when it gets late.
You. Not you, but you who are reading…
what won't you ask for and want?
Of course I remember it differently because I was broke
and it feels like I'm broke still.
The cabs lined up but no one took him
where he wanted to go. Those months shared a face
and the face of a dog on a street was the only thing
that really saw you (for a long time).
Then I heard you were traveling, I heard you were somewhere,
I heard you were nowhere anyone looked for at all.
French stationery. Construction. Sent then deleted. Missed you
so sorry next time press yes to continue press now.
And I stood on Barrow then Greenwich then Allen
then all streets, every street, all the time, everyone.
There was a check you used just to drive out there.
There was a storm that brought a gold door in front of their shoes.
You know, it doesn't get easier with the lights off.
It doesn't get easier to watch the play with an end.
On the way out someone said, what a terrible way to portray life.
But about us. Hide all week then some place
we go empty the dark in. In the dark

with our vices and best shirts and history's dress.
Then you could find me anytime. And then there's right now.
Where wouldn't we go to be no one and those people again?

Alone Together

Where I'm writing this there's an ad for high heaven.
It cost me more than those evenings to see you;
more than a lifetime to see my own face.
Money and time then. Both seem misspent here.
I want the bedroom wall bronze
so I sleep without looking for more.
And a man with his hands on his face is a man.
Nothing solid.
It's hard to believe. Harder yet when we're here
and repeating the same things into the days without grace.
The ocean is old. Planes curve by
and you're back or that's luck,
though not lucky enough to become love.
Or the day in my mother's life
when she forgets (even briefly) about me.
It's not kind to acknowledge affection is finite,
that all kinds of love have to end.
So if cruelty is one side of freedom
we may want to stay free together alone in the thin afternoon.
I can't be here or with you. I know that.
But maybe I'm simple, vicious
and human after all.
When the clocks of this world all go useless with promise,
the coyotes crossing the yard
look beyond us and roam.
We can dine and pretend that our lives
are our lives without speaking.
Fog in the hills.
People stuck in more traffic but moving.
Someone thinking of us. Someone setting the knives.

Together Alone

We may have been alone together
flying over the coast where we both couldn't stay.
The gentleman in the novel came into your bed;
one day, without warning, you felt like him too.
Drawing the shades up, by the door with your hair wet.
When we met, you kept me up saying very few things.
As all else, and dressed wisely, we fled our flawed forms.
Are you surprised then that anyone's staying together? Surprise.
How surprising it turns out to be.
The three of us at twenty or close to the same age.
And no one wore a jacket wherever we went,
like no one wanted love for more than a day.
The boy I buy gin from says *you're next* at just the right moment.
I pay him and slip into touching his hands.
In Bastille—on Sunset—late and blurry in Dolores Park.
What does time have to do with us there?
You ask if charm can redeem someone (maybe),
but none of this runs on logic, and it isn't Voltaire.
At some point they walked in and needed
to throw it away or in someone's way somewhere.
Take your pick, find your match—
it's a real marketplace.
Overlooking Second Avenue I said,
this is one life view. "The delay is temporary."
Over a speaker the sentence repeats like your face.
And I followed you into that temporary;
over the canyons, away from the hills,
far from the ocean and back here.
Toward what felt found and mostly—
it's morning now, nighttime where
you are—was not, would not be.

Bloodless

All day the trees touch each other blindly.
When I pass they don't know I'm going away.
How would you describe the way a person enters a room
they must burn in or swim through?
It's a rumor that anyone lives.
The things that are things, I threw them in boxes.
The things that are mine, I threw them in you.
So he walked from the park, from the past, to the party.
You thought the flowers would like to die with the music on low.
I thought, let some of it live. Let there be people inside there—
turns out just cocktails and language,
another part of the evening, a wind on the river across.
If buzzer is broken, please call.
If stuck, do not push or pull.
He kept pushing until he wasn't himself or you with him.
It's a rumor that anyone gets out in fact.
Once—we saw each other and stayed
in different rooms, like two different countries.
All night I wore your favorite color by mistake.
On the street: voices—"we have a lot of time left."
"All night he looked at me," you said to our friend.
Someone they didn't know spoke loudly and happy.
All the time. All my life. Mostly it's been misleading.
"…And your own life while it's happening…
never has any atmosphere until it's a memory."
To who? Warhol said that, not Proust.
Little remains but it's all here
and I've come to give it to you.
What part to write down in order to tell nothing.
Texts. Emails. No sleep.
And some ink, although bloodless,

marks where you were and they've been.
This was left at the end of the night, this here.
This is what no one wanted to say.

Vacation with Death

Stranger stranger stranger all the money in this world won't work.
And yet, and yet
we wanted our terrible lives.

Every vacation but this one was temporary.
That's us in the photos and us in the bed.
Holidays. First address. Wrong flowers.

I keep a tab and a door open for you.

And the cigarettes smoked in your black sheets.
All that love and the unloved…
strange how strange how strange how it goes.

Water

On a Sunday in Paris a woman is looking for a grave.
We arrived at the hour of champagne flutes,
we were promised a toast so we stayed.
Philip says you won't call like you're needed
so be a calm person in all my dark clothes.
Well, how easy. The curtains part weekly
and the neighbors look in unimpressed.
What is aging exactly?
There are new jobs and people
and someone dies before noon every day.
I am swimming and swimming…in May or an ocean,
I don't see the reason. "But that's unimportant," you said.
"Just keep doing it over again until one day you can't."
Spring excites us and we know what it is every time.
The minutes in meetings are life's most undistinguished;
that's obvious. And what's obvious makes us all fools
then fast friends. One more time then:
What do you do here? Where are you from?
How long are you planning to stay?
A friend tells me how when he leaves for a trip
he sets out a glass of water on the counter of his kitchen.
The woman's still looking. I watch from a bench
and I'm reading a book—she is reading the names.
Faithfully. With much compromise.
I can't tell if it's better than one more French exit today.
So why do you do it, I asked him;
playing my own bartender, taking it down
easy, unlike everything else.
And there's months when I still hear you tell me
"I can't keep anything living."
Not plants. Nothing requiring care.

It's the same glass, only the trips differ.
Something in us needs water so we give it to someone else.

Handsome View of a Lifetime

How despite their secrets it was a handsome view of a lifetime.
The viola player we remembered your street by soon moved.
And I suppose that's how I knew I was happy. I didn't take photos.
The nights were more than our gossip and part of it too.
For the ice to melt, for the bottles to empty—
we seldom saw ourselves in this forecast as brief.
America went on loudly and we stayed here
but listen: scenery, scenery. Matchbooks with one match.
What people wrote to each other in books no one kept.
And your lawyers. They said there were things we can't have back.
The eyes. How they look before we go thinking something.
Past your screen the face of a lover or stranger. What difference.
The monks who were asked what they missed and said
missing was not what they felt. Missing missed them.
It may be enough now to walk in these meaningless rhythms.
Rise, think, undress, repeat.
Each week he spoke to the past with real ceremony.
After years of being next to each other—they met.
Salt covered their bodies, myth took them far west.
"Everyone wants to live," Elizabeth Taylor told Capote.
"Even when they don't want to."
In graveyards and countries where no one's name knows yours.
Where you are most welcome and want to stay least.
The stiff Christmas trees lined each block in that last month.
The New Year's balloons slowly feathered the floors.
And in the daily order…all the laws and the lawless
there was so much no one could ask for.
Why she lived alone in a village of ninety, believe it.
Why you lived as one in a city of crowds. Well, you did.
With its terms of affection, hurried forms of attention
our shameless century tried to find a shorthand for love.

These affairs of ours should only be felt without touching.
But if you sit close enough for a while and do not blink;
you can see they're not dead. Sad to say, we're not saints yet.
We're simply having another and taking it in.

Biography

...or ask the mistakes to give the day texture.
December to seem like July. The sea to make room
and the room to be right here. Language to do more than fill time.

If you forget who you are there's a desk in the afterlife
meant to retrieve you. Yet by some kind of error
(someone told me today), it's been sent and is heavy,
it's been lost on the earth.
I'm no more at home if I'm walking or swimming,
catching an airplane or riding trains backwards
like people of previous years.

This is what he looked like, you said to them,
handing over a photo.
This is how a car drives out of view.
Nothing—not even the nothing—gets written by us.

v

Days and Nights

And every poem with people is for them.
That's how it began: you and me.
How quickly I found myself in the evening.
How slowly Manhattan invited us there.
The past slipped away with the fare and who'd ask for it back?
It so happens you see there were novels and paintings.
Some films and these short days. Then again, we were alone.
Sun and a bit of sand. No money or celebrity
but love for all that it is worth. What you wrote.
When winter found its darkness without us. Of course
there was time and a moon. There was air. All we typed out.
And still. No one knew who we were.
We looked for each other in all of the rooms and their mirrors.
What the champagne couldn't fill. The brief extras and dinners—
so I thought: let love kill us, let it start here.
It's real for them. Even the irony.
When each morning the water hits the back of his neck.
That face. Or the next thought. The next pause.
Someone's cigarette smoke rolling into the street.
And where could they take themselves now (where did we check out)?
If you're asking, it's hardly time to go home.
Because the ticket says here and we arrived at the wrong place.
Painting your walls, letting the wax pool. Thinking of me
and then you. And then you. And then you.
"Mais l'horloge ne sera pas arrivée à ne plus sonner que
l'heure de la pure douleur!"
The handsome child put his hands in the water and his head in the flame.
After all, there was a lot of him left. Anniversaries, birthdays.
How it happened marked an occasion for no one but us.
And I can't stop looking at you when you kneel for the last drawer.
It's late or it's early (to pick out a shirt). So pick out a mood.

Perhaps it's impossible, why anyone goes back for more, he said.

I stopped calling my father and something in me did stop.

Faces of mannequins. Crowds. Capital.

The festival went on for longer than them.

Tried to leave you a note but it's all wind today

and there's more wind tomorrow.

Straighten your tie, throw on those nine o'clock eyes.

What I feel is I'm stopping for you knowing nothing stops for us.

We are here and beginning. In our one misread tongue.

And like that, when I finally arrived there was no one to meet...

looks like we're nothing to look at.

The warmest thing in his house was a book open to page 52.

Past the church doors, away from these engines;

what would it mean if you give up your plan?

On a highway today the spare key found its owner.

We rode the train with a priest without prayer.

With the hundreds of ways to keep something alive

in lost weather. Or call it your body, your home.

When a sentence undoes us faster than money.

Why would we want to know how this ends?

"My life—" wrote Capote, "can be charted as precisely as a fever:

the highs and lows, the very definite cycles."

It's true. We'll all meet each other and soon.

At a different place than we thought. Well past the marked time;

dressed for a happier outcome, they were.

Under the cab light, into the bar talk...

"I can only say, *there* we have been: but I cannot say where."

A new word that could finally address this.

Saw you. Saw no one. Saw nothing.

Saw no thing. Not one thing all fall.

For weeks getting mail for the dead until one of you wrote,

he is dead. Don't you worry about him.

And if it wasn't these grey eyes that had you then: here.

At last—at the start of the hour.
Days and nights at the party.
Nights and days for a price.
It appears, (only now it appears to me)
we've overheard too much to stay young.
How in front of the cameras
it was as if he was seen all the time
for the first time.
What I mean is, who are the people you know you can't love.
Because while the dramas continued the plates under them shifted.
The water rose higher.
Finally they brought in a doctor to discern the small flaw.
Looking back—looks like just sad talk (looks like no more then).
I threw out my hangers and kept all your clothes.
Frames for the savage achievements.
Frames for what cannot be framed.
Hours lost in a car waiting for something to move me.
To pieces. Or the #1 song when you were born.
And what cannot be seen is how chance doesn't talk back.
Spend a life with your debt and your one clue.
Spend it working to work. Spend it spending away.
Old government in the new America.
They want all of your zeros. They want even our nothing.
And when my license expired the same life could see me.
Is it cruel to regret your one body that dies?
By this Union and Waste Land, I'm dazed
but I'm watching the seasons.
And after you leave I lose one of my senses for days.
Again and again. There were malls. Banks.
Years of bombed people.
In the real America with expensive, expendable taste.
"Vite! est-il d'autres vies?"
Please let this go and continue your sentence.

One of these mornings someone may just want to keep you baby
and you'll have to learn new lines for "no."
When you go to parties people ask,
what is it like being with him?
A Malaysian plane disappeared.
Something burned in a field twice.
What is it like being anything then?
And yet, all this happened so I'm trying to reach you
right here in the poem.
Smoking too many cigarettes, writing very few lines.
In the dream we said all we wanted and still took you back.
Without rain their calendars looked like nothing you'd try.
And what about pleasure…
how do you spend it?
Cancel. Cancelled. Cancel.
Ignored and forgotten.
Would I love you more than money?
I did love you and with less.
Whatever your fear is, safe to say that it's coming.
Every night it's all they figured to ask.
When and how often can this be rescheduled?
The far lane turned out to be empty.
He swam alone and heard his own lack.
And everyone has a sixth chapter in their biography.
The beautiful fish rarely live long.
"Then, at one point, I did not need to translate the notes;
they went directly to my hands."
Where underneath the flecked skin
one or one thousand things failed them.
Instead of describing the grass he lay on top of it. Drunk.
Out of the ether, into the graveyard spiral—
if you're thinking of leaving, if you're asking again,
it's hardly time to go home.

So if I'm honest, I'll tell you,

I broke the glass you drink from on purpose.

Possible or unlikely—how Prince Street in early September

has everything anyone wants.

And right now you'll remember

three people who sharply run through you.

"Who is the third who walks always beside you?"

If it's us (and who else), we aren't there. We have fled.

In a comment, under some sort of loss,

a user has written:

"thinking how after twelve years

I came home to find David totally gone.

Car, clothes, accounts. Everything."

Everything in full sun. With speech spilling over it all.

"It's better to hurt people than not to be whole." To Sontag, 1960.

There were portraits of newly made coffins the artist called tests.

Take them with you, he said. As in "to go," if it's urgent.

And why should I care if there's no direct route.

You're in Detroit, San Francisco, Los Angeles,

nighttime. Over the bridge, under the sun.

Not the wires and pills, the announcements or guest lists.

What would we want to power these lives?

In afternoons when they said, *don't forget...*

don't forget what this was on your way out.

Like yards full of metals, like turned earth:

we're stones. We are stones that grey on.

And if you keep your eyes here there's room for a question—

what makes happiness different from anything else?

"Well," said the boy, "I thought we knew more than that."

Here you are. In the wrong shoes at the getting late social.

It's the last person you think of. The first past the alarm.

Soon became every day we attended by promise or boredom.

1955. 1939. 1990.

Tuesday in March. October on Sunday.

If you've been a good host you forget all your lines.

Or, look here and see oil and pencil on pillow.

Your eyes like a hand on Rauschenberg's *Bed*.

It's noon or it's midnight.

An hour in any one language is still just an hour

(it makes the drive longer).

16. 40. 33.

"I go on loving you like water but…"

I go on loving you and going and.

I go on, I go on, I go up.

Unreachable like a live wire in the sky.

We are Pacific, Atlantic, this north or south feeling.

Take the long way forever.

If you're asking, if you still need to know,

it's hardly time to go home.

"Champagne" borrows the opening line, "J'ai plus de souvenirs que si j'avais mille ans," of Charles Baudelaire's poem "Spleen." Joanna Richardson's English translation of this line, "I have more memories than a thousand years," also appears in the poem.

"Cocaine" quotes Lauren Bacall in the line "Who sat on mountaintops in cars reading books aloud to the canyons?"

"The 25th Hour" borrows the line "Exilé sur le sol au milieu des huées," from Charles Baudelaire's poem "L'Albatros." Joanna Richardson's English translation of this line, "Exiled on earth amid the shouting crowds," also appears in the poem.

"The Last Luxury, JFK Jr." borrows lines from a note sent to JFK Jr. from Madonna. It also adapts the second-to-last line of Stephen Spender's poem "The Truly Great" ("Born of the sun, they travelled a short while toward the sun") as its opening line.

"Lindsay Lohan" borrows lines spoken by Marilyn Monroe from *The Making of The Misfits* by James Goode. The line "Her arm was full of bracelets, one of which, she said softly, had been given to her by S" is adapted from *Vanity Fair*'s 2010 profile of Lohan, "Adrift..." by Nancy Jo Sales and Jessica Diehl.

"Elvis in New York" loosely borrows lines from Elvis Presley's press conference at Madison Square Garden on June 9, 1972.

"Some New Thing" adapts the opening lines of Wallace Stevens's "Sunday Morning": "Complacencies of the peignoir, and late / Coffee and oranges..."

"All Apologies" takes its title from the last track on Nirvana's album *In Utero*.

"Central Park" quotes a sentence fragment ("an artificial pastoral in the nineteenth-century English romantic tradition") from Joan Didion's essay "Sentimental Journeys."

"Night Call" was written for a multimedia poetry project of the same name through which I read poems to strangers in bed and online in the months of February and March of 2014. The poem quotes Marilyn Monroe from Truman Capote's conversational portrait "A Beautiful Child."

"Days and Nights" includes lines and quotes from Arthur Rimbaud, Truman Capote, T.S. Eliot, Francesca Woodman, the journals of Susan Sontag, and John Ashbery.

Acknowledgments

Thank you to the editors of the following journals and magazines where some of these poems first appeared, at times in earlier versions: *The Adroit Journal, The American Poetry Review, The Awl, The Baffler, Bennington Review, BOMB, Boston Review, The Brooklyn Rail, Cosmonauts Avenue, Harvard Review, The Journal, Kenyon Review, New England Review, The New York Times Magazine, PEN America, Phantom, Poetry, A Public Space, The Quietus,* and *Salmagundi.*

"Cocaine" was the recipient of a Pushcart Prize.

"Chance Visitors" was written for Jessica Rankin's show *Dear Another,* at Salon 94 in New York City, November through December of 2014.

"In the New Century I Gave You My Name" appeared at *Poetry Daily* on January 24, 2015.

Thank you to everyone at Copper Canyon Press.

Thank you to the sun and the moon.

It means a lot to me to have Francesca Woodman's photograph *Untitled* (Rome, Italy) as the cover of my book. Thank you to the Estate of Francesca Woodman, George and Betty Woodman.

Writing this book coincided with one of the most difficult periods of my life. The work itself was a rescue.

Alex Dimitrov is the author of *Begging for It* and the online chapbook *American Boys*. He lives in New York City.

Poetry is vital to language and living. Since 1972, Copper Canyon Press has published extraordinary poetry from around the world to engage the imaginations and intellects of readers, writers, booksellers, librarians, teachers, students, and donors.

WE ARE GRATEFUL FOR THE MAJOR SUPPORT PROVIDED BY:

THE PAUL G. ALLEN
FAMILY FOUNDATION

TO LEARN MORE ABOUT UNDERWRITING
COPPER CANYON PRESS TITLES,
PLEASE CALL 360-385-4925 EXT. 103

WE ARE GRATEFUL FOR THE MAJOR SUPPORT PROVIDED BY:

Anonymous

Jill Baker and Jeffrey Bishop

Donna and Matt Bellew

John Branch

Diana Broze

Sarah and Tim Cavanaugh

Janet and Les Cox

Catherine Eaton and David E.
     Skinner

Beroz Ferrell & The Point, LLC

Mimi Gardner Gates

Linda Gerrard and Walter Parsons

Gull Industries, Inc.
     on behalf of William and
     Ruth True

Rose Gummow

Steven Myron Holl

Lakeside Industries, Inc.
     on behalf of Jeanne Marie Lee

Maureen Lee and Mark Busto

Rhoady Lee and Alan Gartenhaus

Ellie Mathews and Carl Youngmann
     as The North Press

Anne O'Donnell and John Phillips

Suzie Rapp and Mark Hamilton

Joseph C. Roberts

Jill and Bill Ruckelshaus

Cynthia Lovelace Sears and
     Frank Buxton

Seattle Foundation

Kim and Jeff Seely

Dan Waggoner

Austin Walters

Barbara and Charles Wright

The dedicated interns and
     faithful volunteers of
     Copper Canyon Press

The Chinese character for poetry is made up of two parts:
"word" and "temple." It also serves as pressmark for
Copper Canyon Press.

The poems are set in Fournier. Headings are set in Avenir.
Printed on archival-quality paper.
Book design and composition by Phil Kovacevich.

CPSIA information can be obtained
at www.ICGtesting.com
Printed in the USA
JSHW041821100122
21886JS00005B/5

9 781556 595103